What Remains to Be Seen

poems by

Lauren Rusk

Finishing Line Press
Georgetown, Kentucky

What Remains to Be Seen

Copyright © 2018 by Lauren Rusk
ISBN 978-1-63534-396-0 First Edition
All rights reserved under International and Pan-American Copyright Conventions. No part of this book may be reproduced in any manner whatsoever without written permission from the publisher, except in the case of brief quotations embodied in critical articles and reviews.

Publisher: Leah Maines

Editor: Christen Kincaid

Cover Art: The image of *Kain and Abel* by an unknown artist is from the collections of the Jewish Museum in Prague: Jewish Museum in Prague Photo Archive.

Author Photo: Jamie Clifford

Cover Design: Lauren Rusk and Eric Roberts

Printed in the USA on acid-free paper.
Order online: www.finishinglinepress.com
also available on amazon.com

Author inquiries and mail orders:
Finishing Line Press
P. O. Box 1626
Georgetown, Kentucky 40324
U. S. A.

Contents

Small Child with a Cape 1

What Remains to Be Seen

    In the Balance 5

    Within the Play 6

    Chaos 7

    Invention 8

    Elsewhere 11

    Lessons 14

    A Paper Silhouette 18

    Closing Time, Interstices 19

The People Who Pass By 21

Notes 22

Acknowledgments 24

*To Elisabeth Salisbury
with love and gratitude*

Small Child with a Cape
Hobee's Restaurant, California

Bright-striped Guatemalan cotton—green, russet, and violet
hemmed with clumps of orange tassels—

what were the parents in their drab
windbreakers thinking?

That you can just make a life up
out of whole cloth?

Defenseless child, audacious cape—
this one's out of reach—

What about their own lives, hemmed
by hard work? I can't tell . . .

A girl, or a boy? Across the room
only a round dark head,

a small brown hand,
and the glorious poncho.

Can they really hope this convergence
of earth and fiery wings,

Rivera and Toulouse-Lautrec,
will do the trick?

Look! It's kids-eat-free Wednesday:
the small plate, the clown face

of cantaloupe and berries. Is the divine
infant, as in the old frescoes,

smiling? Or abstracted,
even solemn? The child aflame

with a cloak of many colors
lifts a wondering hand and waits.

~ ~ ~

What Remains to Be Seen

*on children's art
from the ghetto / prison camp Theresienstadt*

In the Balance
    after Edita Pollaková

Not pencil, watercolor! And it's her turn
to sit at the rough table between the bunks,
to be enfolded, borne along
by the woman's voice, "a house.

The essence, a few strokes . . ." What is
a house? This, the girls' barracks
in Terezín, or the farmhouse
they left that night near Branov?

Not *or*— a swath of yellow,
long under the red tile
slanting roof, then a shadowed
wall to make it solid, "safe
as houses," they say in England.

The base of the house is wanting.
She soaks her brush with brown
and paints the line over again,
a stroke that continues
past the building to become

the vein that feeds a leaf, a mere
translucent green ellipse, which the house
stands on, is joined to,

erected ark to impossible leaf, poised
on a wash of sky—
no ground—

only the earthdark veins
she forces through the nearly not there
(verboten)
leaf that holds the house in air.

Within the Play
after Štěpán Pollak

The picture fills with objects, almost none of which
belong in Babylon, where Pyramus and Thisbe
whisper through a garden wall.
The boy who sketches in the barracks

confines them to adjoining houses,
yearning toward each other
from a parlor and a kitchen. Fresh roses,
fresh bread. He's confused—

Pyramus, the image of Walter Raleigh:
a plumed hat, doublet, sword, bouquet;
Thisbe, a young Czech, decorous as a lady
advertising dish detergent.

The summer cardigan, its puffed sleeves.
Her bell-shaped skirt, the zigzag pattern
overlaid with pleats. The bell of her golden hair.
And there behind her, whose milk pitcher,

the line suddenly certain, abides on the shelf?
How he embroiders the *Midsummer Night's Dream*
the elders performed after curfew. Those who,
one on lookout, had to make patches stand for all.

Yet the child ignores the fairies and their fixes.
He homes in on just this scene, this moment.
And omits the foolery, gives no hint
of mechanicals bungling the play

within the play. Their lovers believe themselves,
and so does he. There's no tinker in his picture,
personifying wall. The boy knows what a wall is.

Chaos
    after Raja Engländerová

Fear sweeps her like a broom.
Standing in the cold, the girl shouts without a sound.
A moment ago she prayed to the faces of her fingers,
What can I do.
The useless paws, one still bruised and swollen,
only stared back.
Now she sees nothing.
Not the crowds pushing past,
which the girl above her doesn't draw.
Not the corpse cart, pulled by the nearly dead.
The pencil scours back and forth, merging wall and wind.
In this street the bundled, bound for transport, lurch at night.
Her hair snaps back along the wall, the wind
a stiff hairbrush.
Floating overhead, a heavy door
like all the others. A glowing doorknob.
The curve of her back, shoulder to small,
carves out a question mark.

(All at once I'm there again, the snarling dog's
eyes on my throat, an empty road, nothing
to do but scream to no one, Get your dog away!
When I could see, he was backing off.)

In Terezín, the girl who scrawled a fear
that's hard to tell from anger,
she, and not many others,
drew the long straw out.

Invention
    after Eva Pollenzová

Though some might say she's hardly
da Vinci, Eva likes making pictures.
Art's a game. You plan it out,
use your noggin. First, the theme:
theater in Terezín. Eva knows
right away what she'll draw—
the marionettes!

Rule #1. People consist of basic shapes.
Circles, rectangles, and the triangle,
the wedge, which opens the door
to pyramidal hair, conical hats,
a clown's ruff, stage roof, zigzag valance,
and the princess-in-the-corner's coronet.
Rule #2. Every person is one of a kind.

As Eva draws the scene, each small figure
calls for another. Soon eleven brim
the box, an extra peeking in, the family
flanked by circus folk and royalty,
arranged as in a print Frau Brandeis
showed them from her suitcase.
There's life in it, this box-bound world!

Papa to begin with, huge as a snowman,
his cone hat tilted back as if he's home,
his arms a bridge from mama
to the first-born, who looks Egyptian
with her wedge of curls,
turning her head and feet
to watch the performers.

Her nose grazes the ear of a cat
that stands unsteadily on her shoulder.
For just this detail, this sense
the hand remembers, the line
takes on a sinuous life, the creature's

spine arching, its tail curving
in the air for balance.

They're friends of course,
that's the spark. Everyone's given
someone, some companion.
The jester, a man on stilts;
the princess, a footless boy.
Reaching toward one another
the puppets teeter and sway.

The youngest climb on papa, toppling
about in newspaper hats. Surely
their strings would've tangled!
But Eva's put only one string in,
which holds the jester up, an emblem
of the just-for-show, the ersatz coffee
snatched away as the Red Cross goes.

Nonetheless, how invention flourishes,
when with a freshly sharpened pencil
she layers the littlest actors on,
enhancing the blank-eyed clown
with a trapeze kid, upside-
down—the strings all but forgotten
in the living!

Even before the actors, though, what is it
that catches the eye, and stays in mind?
For me it's structure, the framework
of relation. Eva's people are held together,
built on one another. Whether or not
they touch, the diagonal lines
of their outstretched arms

connect in the eye of the mind.
Like the tall-man bending forward
as he waves a baton, they are all
acrobats. And I've been so caught up,
I overlooked a lone puppet
outside the window, trying
to get some attention.

His hat's too small, like a tea mug,
and he brandishes, what? An ice-cream
cone, a microphone? No, a billy club!
. . . I see, the grasshopper-man on stilts
is miming him back in the corner,
not conducting a symphony!
It's not that kind of baton.

The peeping Tom's a guard, a cop,
on his mark to bust things up,
all those diagonals intersecting,
all that maddening relation
in the cell with triangles fluttering
across the top, drawing the people
together, declaring

this a celebration! . . .
I would like to believe that for Eva too
the man came quite late to the window
that rules him out of bounds,
even as he raises his truncheon
and glares, one might think enviously,
into the overflowing room.

Elsewhere
after Ella Steinová

a squared-off bed with its bolster, built to fit a child's corner,
has risen off the ground, past the trees, and continues to ascend

at the most leisurely of angles, preceded by a nightstand.
The daybed and the nightstand are golden.

It happens even though the youth has grown too long for the bed.
Lying on his belly, an elbow propping his chin, he dangles past
      the footboard.

By *golden*, what I mean is pumpkin overlaid on lemon,
kindled by a blue blanket tucked around the mattress.

The lounging youth gazes at a book held out before him
by a jointed contraption, and absently

guides a kite string, his arm pointing onward.
He can read and fly a kite at the same time!

I say *he* and *his*, but the words don't encompass him.
His pipestem arms, jester's nose, and a look

in his eye, as of something amusing further off,
remind me of the comic Danny Kaye,

whose gender was elusive too, or at least in play.
Oh, but beyond all that, Ella's vision sings with color—

the blue-drenched green of the boy's clothes, vibrant
as the spruces, the crimson of his windrushed hair—

these are colors lush, alive, and grateful,
none unchanged by another, none unechoed.

Red turns to cherry in the pants and slippers
of a man floating overhead, a rabbi

who kicks his candy-striped trousers and curly shoes
in the air, without even a mattress!

—*A rabbi flying, sure! But with such crazy clothes—how do you know
what the fellow is?*—Because like the boy he's a reader too!

Manuscripts dangling from his hands and feet,
another hovering under his eyes, —*Even so,*—

the proper hat, horizontal (although there's no horizon),
and the frock coat, a stout black sailing boat.

—*Okay, granted . . . But if the rabbi's "like the boy,"
aren't "he" and "his" essential, after all?*

As if in response, a few lines emerge
through the watercolor

swirling along the ground.
High-buttoned boots, the barest hint

of a dress, obscured above the waist
—by what? A blue-green cloud?

A sky-filled pond?
In any case, a girl's abandoned

legs are sprinting to catch up.
Now that I've seen her,

the half-penciled girl shadows delight.
I'm drawn by her shoes, one kicking high

after the youth, who thinks as he travels
of something else, of pleasure itself perhaps,

steadied by his blissful friend up ahead.
They pattern themselves after the one above,

the rabbi's companion higher than I can see.
What I can't help seeing, though, beyond the trees

are the youth, the rabbi, and the girl in her boots
all heading toward the prevailing music.

Wait—wouldn't Ella upbraid me for tacking that on?
I can almost hear her—"That's not the story I gave you!

I painted joy. Which hasn't been erased, not altogether."

Lessons
> *after Rudolf Löwy and Mílan Eisler*

"Look, a fistful of pencils, sent by a friend!
Remember school? What was it like,
when you were still allowed?"

~

With the stub closest to hand
Rudolf roughs in a teacher
and the boy she banishes.

Her body's an engine of scribbled sticks
flung into one schematic gesture
that points the way out the door.

Her head's another matter.
There's something of the wailing
Fury about it, the hair rushing back,

an anguished tilt of the brow.
But her mouth, nearly shut,
makes it hard to tell.

What could he have done,
that long-faced boy, whose eyes
turn toward each other in dismay?

He looks like one who wanders
stumbling through the day,
his collar tugged up for him

in the morning, his hair
disheveled since. Surely
his only offense was to live

in his own world.
Now his shoulders have fallen
like a dropped accordion.

Is this the formal expulsion,
the sentinel pointing at his back?
The table like a river divides them.

~

In Mílan's picture, none are banished.
All sorts of boys abound, a scene
of near anarchy. An oblivious

master towers behind his table,
pointing, here too,
but only to prompt a boy

with spectacles like his own.
Upright in his skimpy suit,
the man cleaves to some abstraction,

some absolute. Banners of numerals
unfurl like wings. He seems
not to see unruly children,

even one who sprawls on the floor,
reaching toward a rat. I almost
overlooked him too, a blur

beside the man, whose face
and hand challenge Mílan's
eye and hand. *En garde!*

And there behind the teacher,
a mimic with a crooked smirk
sticks an arm out, brandishing

his chalk. Sharp as a penknife
it tips the master's thigh. *Touché!*
It's harder for Mílan, erasing,

incising, to capture the man.
A chiseled cheek and jaw,
a mildly quizzical brow—

each proud line, balanced
by one that's humble.
Even the overlarge hand

slopes downward as it points,
a languid, reluctant curve
hovering in the air

~

like Adam's in the Sistine Chapel,
where I wondered whether he wants
to partake in all that power.

Yet in both drawings, the teacher raises
the requisite stiff arm, angled upward
to lead the lesson and single out

the pariah. Once, assigned
to sculpt in plaster—a rough
substance that hardens fast—

I built a lecturer tilting forward
and pointing with that same arm,
the one that each of us fears.

Despite some kind professors,
I made mine as top-heavy as the boys',
the arm so overreaching

he would have fallen
without the lectern to prop him up,
listing off true.

~

Why is it that I keep seeing
these two quite different boys
as one—their pictures, a diptych?

Rudolf's driven to feel again
the chaos in the body
when you know you're cast out,

and Mílan dares that moment
to come on—what the hell
is he thinking?

Each of them, remembering
how he wanted to find a place,
draws right up to disaster.

What kinds of lessons must they have faced?
Grasping a pencil, perhaps they answer.

What would exile mean, if not to sever love?

A Paper Silhouette
after an unnamed child

The fallen, the uppermost:
two men hacked from a single
rock, a blind white flash

against grass green. Say it's a boy
who struggles the interlocked
figures from the page.

The tiller's back curves as he bends
over his brother, who strains up
from the ground, still refusing to yield.

Though Cain's the elder son
he looks like a stripling,
grabbing his brother's shoulder

to hold him down 'til he gives.
Or instead is he tugging, trying
to make him stand again?

Slowing the headlong shears,
the boy wills the blades
to find a shape that answers,

a human shape, as of two
becoming one, to emblazon
the grass-green desert.

His hand, half closing, judders
against the paper, the scissors,
the never-ending rock.

Closing Time, Interstices

They've done a kindness, these brief children. So too, the path by which we have to leave, winding through an old graveyard. The stones, themselves a ghetto, incline to one another. Those in Terezín who thronged the squares, waiting for soup, for something, and those who could no longer descend the stairs are not the ones layered here. Yet it holds them. High, light-admitting maples filter summer dust to shades of green. Up close, the weathered stone's not gray but lichened—olive, rose, and whitened taupe, streaked and stained as ancient maps, ourselves bereft and wandering. How can I leave them, these children alive in their moment of making?

The People Who Pass By
Oxford, March 21, 2003

They flow around us, our vigil a stone
in their stream, where High and Cornmarket
meet under an ancient clock.

One by one we mostly can't be heard
protesting the bombs, falling now
on Iraq. It's six p.m., the light

lasting longer. Speakers' heads like horses'
shy away from the microphone.
I lean in to hear them say, we must

not kill. Students in turbans, gauze
tunics wafting, lean in too,
as each quarter hour drowns

a voice. Mechanical soldiers, Romans
freshly painted, hammer out the time.
And teenagers crouch on a doorstep, strumming

as if this were a festival. The river of people
surges on, accustomed to vigils, guitars,
mallets, and bells. What are they all doing

that's so important? Eating a bap.
Swinging a bag of fuchsia tissue paper
from the Oasis, some boutique.

Pulling a trolley of odds and ends,
perhaps to give the Oxfam shop. Or there,
leaning against the wall of that bakery,

breathing in. Shifting a headscarf to cover
an errant tendril, or tilting a daughter's
pram up and over the curb,

apologizing, laughing, getting along,
quenching, lifting us, tumbling our edges—
the source, the wellspring, our unvoiced song.

Notes

What Remains to Be Seen
The labor camp Theresienstadt, in the town of Terezín near Prague, held Jewish people whom the Nazis wanted the world to believe they treated well—the elderly, veterans, artists, scientists, diplomats, and intellectuals, along with their families. In fact, the ghetto was a transit station from which inmates were secretly shipped to Auschwitz. Many died beforehand from overwork, hunger, cold, disease, and sadistic treatment. Others were imprisoned nearby, tortured, and executed. In the ghetto, people were allowed to manage their lives beyond work to some degree, though with severe constraints. They bolstered one another's spirits by giving lectures and putting on concerts, cabarets, plays, and operas, often illicitly. Prisoners employed to create propaganda for the Reich risked their safety to steal and share supplies. After work, artists wrote, composed, and painted, and the children published features and poems in their own newspapers. Thanks to the artist Friedl Dicker-Brandeis, who devoted herself to teaching art to the children, two suitcases of their pictures were discovered behind a wall after the war ended. Many are on view at the Pinkas Synagogue, part of the Jewish Museum in Prague.

Though informed by accounts of other inmates at Theresienstadt, I could only imagine through their pictures the young artists whose work inspired these poems.

In the Balance
The painting is reproduced in *Friedl Dicker-Brandeis* by Elena Makarova and Regina Seidman Miller (Los Angeles: Tallfellow/Every Picture Press, 2001, p. 199).

Invention
For an inspection by the International Red Cross, the Nazis spruced up the camp, shipped off the dying, installed fake cafés and shops, ordered performances of music and sport, and made sure the visitors didn't stray from their route. The hoax yielded a favorable report. The Reich then made a public-relations film in which the fittest-looking captives were forced to act happy and fulfilled in their "spa town."

Elsewhere
Danny Kaye (1913-87) was an American comic actor, singer, and dancer who became an ambassador-at-large for UNICEF in 1954.

Lessons
The acute accent on *Mílan*, not conventional, is included to indicate the stress on the first syllable in Czech.

A Paper Silhouette
The words *as of two becoming one* are drawn from "Of Modern Poetry" by Wallace Stevens.

Closing Time, Interstices
The graveyard is the Old Jewish Cemetery next to the Pinkas Synagogue in Prague.

The People Who Pass By
Oxfam is an international association working to end global poverty and injustice. Initially called the Oxford Committee for Famine Relief, it was founded in England in 1942.

Acknowledgments

First to those whom I can't thank enough for their care and insight, let me try. To Mark Doty, I am immensely grateful for your engagement with the Terezín project and your helping me find my way to the end. To Elisabeth Salisbury, sharing the poems with you has heartened and enlightened me all along. And especially to Eric Roberts, your understanding and love have made possible this journey of exploration, making, and—you among all know how much—remaking.

The project has been blessed with kind supporters. At the outset, Leslie Ullman encouraged me to write about Theresienstadt and suggested books that brought the history to life. A John Woods Scholarship for study in Prague enabled my first trip to Terezín. For the second visit, Karen Kramer, Director of Stanford's program in Germany, sent me off with her own folding seat to camp in front of the children's pictures, and then arranged a writing residency in Berlin. Likewise Geoffrey Tyack, Director of Stanford in Oxford, enabled me to do research at the Bodleian Library while living in Stanford's faculty flat. And later the Vermont Studio Center provided space and time to develop the poems. Many thanks to you all.

Special thanks as well to friends and colleagues who made the work this chapbook represents feel worthwhile at crucial moments: Felicity Allbrooke, Alan Allport, Virginia Allport, Nathalie Anderson, Judith Barrington, Beverly Bie Brahic, Nancy Brink, Thea Cohen, C. W. Emerson, Michael Faletra, Jonathan Farmer, Karen Head, Ursula Howard, Jeffrey Levine, Annie Lighthart, Naomi Major, Max Maxwell, Katherine McNamara, Paul Merchant, Philip Metres, William Olsen, Nancy Packer, Emma Schofield, Sofia Starnes, Penny Tyack, Victoria Van Hyning, Rhett Watts, Merryn Williams, and Stephen Yeo.

And to its publisher Leah Maines, its editor Christen Kincaid, and all the conscientious, thoughtful people at Finishing Line Press, my gratitude for bringing this collection to light.

Finally, I am grateful for the following publications and honors. "The People Who Pass By" appears in the anthologies *Come Together: Imagine Peace* (US) and *Infinite Riches in a Little Room* (UK), and the Terezín sequence was published in *Long Poem Magazine* (UK). The Poetry Society of Virginia awarded a prize to "Small Child with a Cape," and an earlier version of *What Remains to Be Seen* was short-listed for the Munster Literature Centre's International Fool for Poetry Prize.

Lauren Rusk's poems and essays have appeared in *Best New Poets* (winning the Open Competition Prize), *Hotel Amerika*, *The Wallace Stevens Journal*, the *Writer's Chronicle*, and elsewhere. Her books are the poetry collection *Pictures in the Firestorm* (2nd edition 2015) and a critical study, *The Life Writing of Otherness: Woolf, Baldwin, Kingston, and Winterson*. She earned a bachelor's degree at Reed College, an MFA in poetry at Vermont College of Fine Arts, and a doctorate at Stanford University. She has also taught at Stanford, including its programs in Paris, Oxford, and Berlin, and at Swarthmore College, as well as A Room of Her Own Foundation's retreat. Beyond Stanford, she divides her time between Portland, Oregon, and Oxford, England.

Early endeavors include tending bar in El Paso at the Linger Inn, weaving voices through the dark as a long-distance operator, learning from and sometimes teaching three- to six-year-olds, sketching cats, then people, sneaking around and keeping still, singing to the ceiling, and reading through the night.

www.ingramcontent.com/pod-product-compliance
Lightning Source LLC
LaVergne TN
LVHW041518070426
835507LV00012B/1661